Interviewing Yourself and Asking the Right Questions

Interviewing Yourself and Asking the Right Questions

Learning What Your Answers Point To

Brent M. Jones

Published by
Connected Events Matter

"Interviewing Yourself and Asking the Right Questions:

Learning What Your Answers Point To

© 2023 Brent M. Jones

Published by Connected Events Matter

© Copyright 2023 Connected Events Matter

www.connectedeventsmatter.com

Contents

Introduction

What questions should you ask yourself to avoid being stuck in a repetitive or negative cycle? Here is a tip to consider. Remember that last important job interview when the first question is, "Tell me about yourself." Of course, in that setting, your answers will want to focus on the parts of you that fit their job opening because they are trying to see if you fit.

Use this same approach on yourself.

Take an honest long look at yourself and then tell yourself about "you". List on paper the good and not so good. If you approach this right, it will indeed tell you whether you're just spinning your wheels as well as where you fit and don't fit.

__Interviewing yourself, asking the right questions, and then understanding what your answers mean is a goal for this book.__

This is a starting place for making changes and preparing for the steps that change will require.

This approach is also about placing accountability for achieving your goals on you, enabling you to come face-to-face with what needs improvement. By looking within, you will find if you're willing to embrace both the best and worst aspects of yourself and then accept who you are in this life.

Going inside means you process information based on what you believe, think, feel, and what your intuitive senses tell you.

This inner place is your life force. It is your consciousness. It has no physical form, but it is your spiritual core, nature, inner self, and essence of who you are.

Some people are conscious of an inner voice that combines conscious thoughts with one's essence of beliefs and biases, a filter processing each day's experiences. This internal monologue, for many, is a natural process and is a way we talk to ourselves.

This little voice in our head is where our Interview of Self begins. We can ask ourselves what a conversation means or interpret details to interpret what happened.

These thoughts are essential in understanding ourselves and the world around us. We create our reality with what we think and often what we think are in what our questions are. We choose how we see and what we question about the world, the people we meet, and ourselves.

Our inner voice may be telling us to seek a change in our lives, but we need to understand why that change will help us and what the change will be.

"You need a change, but you need to change to get that".

Chapter 1: Change Begins as a Thought

A Thought

If you want to change your life, start with your thoughts and the questions your thoughts present. Write down your thoughts and ask yourself questions about them. It's common to want to change but struggle to break out of familiar patterns of thoughts leading to the same results.

Did you know that 90% of your thoughts today are the same ones you had yesterday's? This can keep you stuck in the same behaviors and routines. Instead, you must shift your mindset and think about new things to transform or even better think about finding answers to those questions you already have in your thoughts.

It's more than just waiting for external circumstances to change. Real change comes from within. It is essential to find out our thoughts and tie them to our goals because they have a powerful impact on our behavior and actions. By understanding our thoughts, we can identify any negative self-talk or limiting beliefs that may be holding us back from achieving our goals. Once we have identified these thoughts and the questions they present, we can work on shifting our mindset using affirmations and visualization. By tying our thoughts to our goals, we create a powerful sense of motivation and purpose that can help us stay focused and committed to achieving our desired outcomes. Ultimately, the key to success lies in our ability to control our thoughts and beliefs and use them to create the life we truly want.

Knowing where to start when making changes in your life can be overwhelming. The good news is that you can start small by focusing on your thoughts. As mentioned earlier, our thoughts have a powerful impact on our behavior and actions. By changing how we think, we can change how we live our lives.

One effective way to shift your mindset is using affirmations. Affirmations are positive statements you repeat daily to reprogram your subconscious mind by adding new thoughts. They can combat negative self-talk, boost your confidence, and help you achieve your goals.

For example, if you struggle with self-doubt, you could use an affirmation like "I am confident and capable." Repeat this statement to yourself every morning and throughout the day as needed. Over time, your subconscious mind will start to believe this statement, and you will begin to feel more confident and capable in your daily life.

Another effective way to shift your mindset is using visualization. Visualization is creating mental images of what you want to achieve or experience. Visualizing yourself and achieving your goals can create a powerful motivation and purpose.

For example, if you want to lose weight, you could visualize yourself at your ideal weight, feeling confident and healthy. For instance, you could imagine enjoying healthy meals and engaging in your desired physical activity. By visualizing this outcome, you can create a sense of excitement and motivation to act on your goal.

Remember, real change comes from within. Focusing on your thoughts and mindset can transform your life in powerful ways. It may take time and effort, but the results are worth it. Start small and be consistent, and you will see positive changes in your life.

Chapter 2: The Question to Ask Yourself and Why

Sometimes people have goals they are working towards a step at a time, resulting in reaching a goal or finding their dream job. Other times you may find that your goals and the idea of a dream job is looking for a way out of a place you don't want to be.

The dream or goal might be the perceived job or change, but it, in most cases, it is finding the way out of what they don't like about what they're doing. Since most people quit companies because of how their supervisors treat them, they may look for their dream supervisor or boss rather than a different job. However, knowing how to identify your goals is a process that can be found by interviewing yourself.

For example, working as a career counselor, it has been common to hear people say they are looking for, or hoping to find, their dream job someday. It isn't unusual to find someone who has been in a particular job sector for a long time saying they want something different in their next job. They are fed up or even burned out and think they will enjoy a change. They believe they need to find something different from what they have been doing or something they have always dreamed of doing. They might have left their prior employment because of not being treated fairly, but they would instead look for people who will be positive and fair they look for a completely different job, expecting the people to all be different since, after all, dreams are good things.

As a career counselor, asking a simple question sometimes brings the expectations back to reality. I have found that this happens by asking if it is okay if they make half the money since their previous job history and skills won't lead them to the dream job category they have identified.

Most people, especially if they are a little older, already understand that, but it helps to suggest that some of their recent experience can open them up to different positions and kinds of companies that might be dream jobs.

Finding solutions for these situations requires getting the person to see themselves from a broader perspective and understand more about what they want and why they want it. These answers come from contracting a person to see themselves more clearly and showing that the process involves answering the right questions. If they knew the questions, they wouldn't need a career advisor and would be well on their way to solving their problem.

Chapter 3: Questions to Ask Yourself

Self-awareness is a key component of success. This is not something new. It is a concept that has been around for thousands of years. The Greek philosopher Aristotle, who lived between 384 and 322 BC, once said:

"Knowing yourself is the beginning of all wisdom."

Make a list of questions that will point to who you are. Write them down. Make sure the list includes what you are good, average, or bad at. It can help to show the things that you're good at whether you love, like or don't like doing them.

It will help make things clearer if you divide these findings into several lists. One for things you love and are good at. One for things you hate this and are good or maybe bad at it. These lists will help point you in the right direction enabling you to understand yourself better and find changes that will help.

On each of the lists rank them with the top ones being the strongest one. This can include the I don't like doing this "the most" being on top.

Key Questions to Ask

1. What am I good at?

2. What do I hate doing?

3. What am I just average at doing?

4. What would I like if I had more training?

5. What job have I been the most successful at?

6. What am I bad at?

7. What makes me tired?

8. What is the most important thing in my life?

9. Who are the most important people in my life?

10. How much sleep do I need?

11. What stresses me out?

12. What relaxes me?

13. What's my definition of success?

14. What type of worker am I?

15. How do I want others to see me?

16. What makes me sad?

17. What makes me happy?

18. What makes me angry?

19. What type of person do I want to be?

20. What type of friend do I want to be?

21. What do I think about myself?

22. What things do I value in life?

23. What makes me afraid?

24. Do I like working on a team

25. Do I prefer working alone

1. List of Positive Findings Ranked

From the key question list make a new list of those things you like and are good and would have a positive influence on you and rank them.

2. List All of Your Skills and Concerns

Make a skills list that includes all your skills including hard skills and soft skills and rank them based on your preference (ones you really like doing) and ability. As part of these lists or separately list things you have really liked about your career and associates.

To find the best career fit will require that our skills fit that career needs. By asking yourself these questions, you will find the answers you value rather than ones you may only guess are best. Revealing the real answers about yourself will result in a more authentic presentation when you are asked about yourself.

The list might include:

- Hard and Soft Skills that are used both at work and in daily life.
- Skills you are very good at and haven't had the opportunity to use.
- Mistreatment by immediate supervisor.
- Company policies that you do not approve of.

- Lack of financial incentives or potential growth.

- Narrow focus where it was clear you could do more.

- The location of employment is too far away.

- Employment requires too much travel.

- Employment is short term.

- Few or maybe no benefits.

- A feeling that you're ready for more responsibility.

- Lack of opportunities for professional growth and development.

- Work environment that isn't best suited for you.

- A skill you'd like to learn or knowledge base you'd like to build but can't in your current role.

Using lists #1 and #2 will show you where you fit. If your current situation is in conflict with the top ranked items on these lists it will show you what you need to change.

Chapter 4: Your Skills and Preferences are Part of Who You Are.

Creating the lists mentioned in Chapter 3 is a way to help find out who you are. These are questions you ask yourself. They are the right questions because as you review and update them and rank them according to skill and preference it helps you get on the right path.

If you spend 40 hours a week working for 50 weeks a year you are spending 2000 hours a year. If you sleep 8 hours a day, then you spend 2,912 hours a year sleeping. A year has 8,760 hours so your non-working awake time is 3848 total hours.

If you have many skills ranked high, and those skills are not included in your most recent job description or regular awake hour activities, then that confirms your problem and points to a direction to solve it.

What Can You Learn from an Interview with Yourself

Sometimes you must dig more profoundly than just identifying all the things you like best, so hopefully, you can find a better opportunity with the list as a search tool to determine the better fit.

Rather than just knowing what you like best or least still leaves unanswered questions about why that is the case. For example, finding out why you don't like being responsible for the cash might point you in a new direction. If you feel tempted by the money or comprised by those asking for trust, then that can be a tip-off to other job titles or even the use of skills you want to have on the bottom of your like list.

Self-questioning can help you break through being emotionally stuck. After determining that you are stuck, you can ask yourself the simple but complex question, "Why am I emotionally stuck?" You may answer, "I am emotionally stuck because I have lost the ability to feel any sadness, anger, or joy.

Conducting a self-interview can be a powerful tool for self-reflection and personal growth. By asking yourself questions and answering them honestly, you can gain valuable insights into your thoughts, feelings, and behaviors.

Here are some of the things you can learn from conducting a self-interview:

1. Self-awareness: When you ask yourself questions, you must think deeply about your answers. This process can help you become more self-aware. For example, you may uncover hidden beliefs, biases, or emotions you weren't unaware of. By understanding yourself better, you can make more informed decisions and improve your relationships with others.

2. Clarity: Sometimes, we need help making decisions because we need clarification on what we want. Conducting a self-interview can help you clarify your goals, values, and priorities by asking yourself questions like "What do I want?" or "What's most important to me?" you can clarify what you want to achieve in your life.

3. Problem-solving: When you face a problem, talking about it with someone else can be helpful. But a self-interview can be a great alternative if you don't have anyone to talk to. By asking yourself questions like "What are my options?" or "What's the worst that could happen?", you can brainstorm solutions and devise a plan of action.

4. Self-acceptance: Sometimes, we're our own worst critics. We judge ourselves harshly and focus on our flaws and shortcomings. Conducting a self-interview can help you practice self-compassion and self-acceptance by asking yourself questions like "What am I proud of?" or "What have I accomplished?"

Conducting a self-interview can be valuable for personal growth and self-reflection. You can gain self-awareness, clarity, problem-solving skills, and self-acceptance by asking and answering questions honestly. So next time you feel stuck or unsure, try conducting a self-interview and see what you can learn about yourself.

The first four chapters of this book require you to interview yourself. Your answer shows your skills and abilities and ranks them from those you are best at to those you like doing the most. Chapter 3 reveals the experiences that you want in your work. Chapter 5 shows how you can use this information in a job search.

The skills, abilities, and experiences list will point to a career or specific job. That is your dream job based on your experience and current abilities.

Chapter 5: Interviews are a Two-way Street.

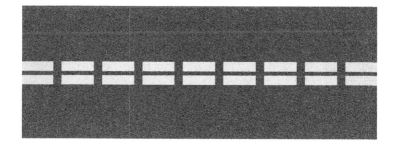

To learn about a supervisor may require you to ask questions to past employees or if possible current employees. It is a good example of the importance of who and where you focus your questions.

A caring boss is highly valued by their employees, while a boss who neglects their team is often disliked. Many workers leave their jobs because of poor relationships with their bosses rather than issues with the company. This suggests that a good boss is more important than a good company regarding job satisfaction.

As a potential employee, you should research the boss's past direct reports on LinkedIn to gain insight into what working for them is like. Additionally, ask questions that reveal the boss's core values and what they look for in a team member. A good boss will foster an environment of integrity, trust, and respect while encouraging innovation, creativity, and feedback. Employees who work in such an environment typically perform at their best. When finding a good boss, it's essential to consider their leadership style and communication skills. A boss who is open and transparent with their team about company goals, expectations, and challenges will likely build stronger relationships with their employees. This, in turn, can lead to higher levels of employee satisfaction, productivity, and engagement.

One way to gauge a boss's communication style is to observe how they interact with their team during the interview process. A good boss will listen actively, ask thoughtful questions, and provide clear and concise feedback. They will also be willing to answer any questions you have about the company culture, team dynamics, and job responsibilities. For example, suppose a boss seems disengaged, dismissive, or uninterested in your questions. In that case, it may be a red flag that they must be invested in building a positive working relationship with their employees.

Another critical factor to consider when evaluating a boss is their ability to provide constructive feedback and support. A good boss will offer regular feedback on your performance, identify areas for improvement, and provide resources and guidance to help you grow professionally. They will also be receptive to your feedback and suggestions and work collaboratively with you to achieve shared goals.

Of course, finding a good boss is only half the battle. As an employee, taking ownership of your career development and seeking opportunities to learn and grow is essential. This may involve seeking additional training or education, volunteering for new projects, or taking on leadership roles within your team. By demonstrating your commitment to personal and professional growth, you can build a strong working relationship with your boss and position yourself for long-term success within the company.

Ultimately, a good boss prioritizes the well-being and development of their employees. They will provide clear direction, offer regular feedback, and foster an environment of trust, respect, and collaboration. By taking the time to research potential bosses and ask thoughtful questions during the interview process, you can increase your chances of finding a boss who will help you achieve your career goals and build fulfilling and rewarding care.

Chapter 6: What Can You Learn from Being Interviewed

Overall, asking questions during an interview is an essential part of the process. It helps you gather information, assess fit, demonstrate your interest, and leave a positive impression on the interviewer.

Asking Questions is a Skill

To acquire knowledge.

To eliminate confusion.

To cause someone else to feel special/important.

To guide a conversation in the direction we want it to go.

To demonstrate humility to another.

To enable a person to discover answers for themselves

To gain empathy through better understanding another's view

To influence or alter someone else's opinion

To begin or strengthen a relationship.

To stimulate creativity and idea generation

To gain a person's attention

To solve a problem

Interviewing yourself is also an effective way to organize your thoughts, control anxiety and push yourself on towards a goal.

Asking yourself the right kind of questions can bring you closer to who you are now, and who you want to be. Think of it as a mirror into your innermost desires, goals and hopes. The ones you didn't even know you had.

Chapter 7: Why Your Past Self Is Holding You Back from Your Future Success

Do you ever feel like you're stuck in the past? No matter how hard you try, you can't seem to move forward. If so, you're not alone. Many people struggle with the limitations of their past selves. But the good news is that there are ways to overcome these obstacles and unlock your full potential for personal reinvention.

This chapter will explore why your past self may be holding you back and how to break free from those limitations. From the power of the past to the benefits of personal reinvention, we'll provide you with a roadmap to achieve tremendous success in the future. So, if you're ready to leave your past behind, keep reading.

One of the reasons it can be challenging to break free from the limitations of our past selves is that change is hard. Our brains are wired to resist change and to stick to familiar patterns and behaviors, even when they no longer serve us. This natural defense mechanism is designed to keep us safe but can also hold us back from achieving our full potential. So how do we overcome this resistance to change? Stay tuned for insights on the power of embracing discomfort and stepping outside of our comfort zones.

Why change is hard?

One of the biggest challenges in breaking free from the limitations of our past selves is the inherent difficulty of change. Our brains are wired to seek familiarity and resist anything that disrupts the status quo, even if it is ultimately beneficial. This resistance can manifest as fear, procrastination, or rationalizations that keep us from taking risks or trying new things.

However, it's essential to recognize that change is necessary and inevitable in life. The world constantly evolves, and we must adapt and grow to avoid becoming stagnant and irrelevant. Embracing the discomfort and stepping outside of our comfort zones can be uncomfortable, but it's often where the most significant opportunities for growth and transformation lie.

So, while it may be hard to break free from the limitations of our past selves, it's important to remember that change is possible and essential for our personal and professional success. In the next section, we'll explore some practical strategies for overcoming the resistance to change and unlocking our full potential.,

How to overcome the limitations of your past self

To overcome the limitations of our past selves, we need to start by acknowledging that change is an inevitable part of life. The world constantly evolves; if we adapt and grow, we avoid becoming stagnant and irrelevant. So, embracing discomfort and pushing ourselves outside our comfort zones is essential.

One strategy for overcoming resistance to change is focusing on personal reinvention benefits. When we take risks and try new things, we expand our skills and knowledge, which can lead to exciting opportunities and personal growth. It's natural to feel apprehensive about stepping into the unknown, but by reframing our mindset and focusing on the potential rewards, we can find the motivation to move forward.

Another way to overcome the limitations of our past selves is to seek out new experiences and perspectives. This can involve trying new hobbies, traveling to different places, or connecting with people with diverse backgrounds and viewpoints. Exposing ourselves to new ideas and ways of thinking can broaden our horizons and challenge our assumptions.

Ultimately, breaking free from the limitations of our past selves requires a willingness to take risks and embrace change. It can be uncomfortable initially, but by staying open-minded and motivated, we can unlock our full potential and achieve incredible personal and professional growth. In the next section, we'll explore the benefits of personal reinvention in more detail.,

The benefits of personal reinvention

Personal reinvention has numerous benefits that can positively impact our lives. We can create a more fulfilling and meaningful existence by embracing change and seeking new experiences. One of the most significant advantages of personal reinvention is increased self-awareness. When we take the time to reflect on our past selves and identify areas for improvement, we become more in tune with our values, strengths, and weaknesses. This self-awareness can lead to better decision-making and a stronger sense of purpose.

Personal reinvention can also lead to increased creativity and innovation. By exposing ourselves to new experiences and perspectives, we can generate fresh ideas and approach challenges in new ways. This can be especially valuable in our professional lives, where creativity and innovation are highly valued.

Furthermore, personal reinvention can improve our relationships with others. As a result, we become more empathetic and understanding by broadening our horizons and challenging our assumptions. This can lead to stronger connections with friends, family, and colleagues and increased opportunities for collaboration and teamwork.

Summing up these thoughts: personal reinvention can unlock our full potential and lead to incredible personal and professional growth. By embracing change and seeking out new experiences, we can increase self-awareness, creativity, and empathy, ultimately leading to a more fulfilling and meaningful life.,

In addition, our past experiences can act as shackles, hindering us from achieving our true potential. However, we can unlock our full potential for personal reinvention by understanding the power of the past, recognizing why change is hard, and taking proactive steps to overcome our past limitations.

Such reinventions have numerous benefits, including increased happiness, improved productivity, and tremendous success.

So, begin today and start creating the future you deserve because, as Henry David Thoreau said,"

*"Go confidently in the direction of your dreams!
Live the life you've imagined."*

Chapter 8: First See Yourself Correctly and Then Reinvent Yourself

The decision to reinvent yourself will require you to see yourself correctly first. To answer the question, "Who are you" requires seeing your past and present, and both views can be a challenge to determining what you want as the result of your reinvention of self.

Your past and current goals and desires

influence the direction you have decided to take. It may seem positive to change and define yourself in terms of plans you have not reached yet, but that can be a trap. It can cause you to lose sight of who you are right now. This will lead to your skipping over correcting what created the previous poor choices. Making better choices is just as important as setting reasonable goals.

Reinventing yourself requires you to learn from each new step you take. Looking back at your past from the present will show past actions in a new, more experienced light, which is how reinvention begins.

Examining past choices and the changes they brought about shows the reinvention process and suggests your next steps.

Changing yourself only takes place if you have identified your strengths and weaknesses. Knowing your strengths and weaknesses, from your relationships to those in your career.

Self-assessment and seeing yourself outside of yourself help you better understand what you seek and where you will likely thrive and excel. It gives you a better understanding of your desire and where you will probably do well.

Making the right changes enables you to become the person you want to be. Practicing and enacting change yourself is one of the most rewarding processes you will ever experience. It also displays a particular life skill, the ability to reinvent yourself.

Quotes about Reinvention

1. "It's never too late to be what you might have been." -- George Elliot

2. "When I let go of what I am, I become what I might be." -- Lao Tzu

3. "The reinvention of daily life means marching off the edge of our maps." -- Bob Black

4. "Change your life today. Don't gamble on the future; act now, without delay." -- Simone de Beauvoir

Self-improvement only takes place if you have identified your strengths and weaknesses. You know your strengths and weaknesses, from your relationships to those in your career.

Self-assessment and seeing yourself outside

of yourself help you better understand what you seek and where you will likely thrive and excel. It gives you a better understanding of your desire and where you will probably do well.

Change enables you to become the person you want to be. Practicing and enacting change yourself is one of the most rewarding processes you will ever experience. It also displays a particular life skill, the ability to reinvent yourself.

Chapter 9: Storytelling Helps Us Construct Our Identity.

The stories reveal how we think, what we feel, and how we justify our decisions. We see ourselves and our experiences as part of the totality of human experience. Retelling our story can create stronger emotions that serve as markers for the future retrieval of the events. The recollections and feelings continue to shape us long after the events they represent have passed.

The recollections, feelings, and emotions attached to events have their power. They become the entry points to a changing perspective of the world.

Your personality is your identity. It is you and no one else. A combination of behaviors, emotions, thought patterns, and motivations defines you. For example, it might be said that your genetics, the environment you're in, and the influence of your peers is the personality. Those factors would be accurate, but to identify what they have created, one can listen to a person's stories, and the result of those influences are evident.

"Life stories do not simply reflect personality. They are personality, or more accurately, they are important parts of personality, along with other parts, like dispositional traits, goals, and values," writes Dan McAdams, a professor of psychology at Northwestern University, along with Erika Manczak, in a chapter for the APA Handbook of Personality and Social Psychology.

Why do the stories change so much over time? When retelling the story, why does a person draw a different conclusion about events? For example, a study at Columbia University by B. Tversky concluded that "When people retell events, they take different perspectives for different audiences and purposes.

Another study by the National Library of Medicine by Nat Rev Neurosci in 2014 titled "The Neuroscience of Memory: Implications for the Courtroom" concluded that memory can sometimes be hazy. Over time, distortions in memory occur through the influence of other witnesses to the events or the results of our own bias. Memories change with age, how the event was experienced, or even just lost on a molecular level.

What doesn't change is that an event shapes us; as our memories change, the shape we have taken from those influences' changes.

What we have always considered a life-changing event is reinforced with emotion and trauma. Time may reveal different influences than what was first thought. Still, the emotion and trauma continue to make the evolving conclusions that could take place to the person impacted in the beginning. The exact original data is reinforced by different decisions driven by the emotions that have made the event necessary in the first place.

Chapter 10: Why Does My Story Matter?

Our life story represents our perception of reality and is the lens through which we view it. These perceptions influence how we focus on, interpret, remember, and act on the truth.

Your life story and how you see it also enable you to understand other people's experiences better. For example, when you alter the narrative about what you thought was reality, you're telling yourself that the new perceptions will change you and often enable you to take steps forward proactively based on what may be considered a more experienced narrative.

Some believe older adults make better decisions because they look at the whole picture. That also means they have changed their conclusions about the facts of various events when reconsidering similar new events.

Your stories let you share information in a way that creates an emotional connection.

Becoming aware of our stories has utility beyond personal development and is usable in everyday interactions. We share our life stories in small talk: "Hi, where are you from?" "Where did you grow up?" "Which school did you attend?"

"How you arrange the plot points of your life into narrative shapes says who you are and is a fundamental part of being human," said Monisha Pasupathi, a professor of developmental psychology at the University of Utah, in her 2015 article in The Atlantic, "Life's Stories." "To have relationships, we've all had to tell little pieces of our story."

The power of personal stories is vital in establishing relationships, even in those cases where a motive is a driving force. Successful salespeople reach out to develop a working relationship with customers to demonstrate familiarity, create trust and communication, and help customers feel more secure and connected.

A store clerk mentions where she grew up in a conversation about a product you are discussing, and you know someone who grew up there, or perhaps you did. You mention the street, and the clerk says having once lived a few blocks away. Each shared parts of your personal story, resulting in a small bond.

People want to connect and share some of their stories because sharing stories is the only way we can connect as humans. Learning more about someone and their story enables us to understand them differently and form a deeper connection.

"When someone shows you who they are, believe them the first time".

-- Maya Angelo

Chapter 11: Why Other People's Stories Matter

"A reader lives a thousand lives before he dies, said Jojen." "The man who never reads lives only one. - George R.R. Martin, A Dance with Dragons."

You thought about how your personal story made you who you are today. But you don't live on an island. To learn what makes you human necessitates more than looking inward. You must also be curious to find other points of view. Different perspectives shine a light on our own lives.

Art, music, poetry, literature, service to others, and even food can influence us to the point where they can become part of our life story. Since humans are social animals, our lives comprise several influences that construct how we see the world. It informs us how we view our surroundings and various roles within our family, friends, and community.

Author Tony Hillerman wrote about the Navajo people, "Everything is connected. The wing of the corn beetle affects the direction of the wind, the way the sand drifts, and the way the light reflects into the eye of a man beholding his reality. All are part of totality; in this totality, man finds his hero, his way of walking in harmony, with beauty all around him." (HOZRO: the Navajo word meaning to be in harmony with one's environment, at peace with one's circumstances, free from anger or anxieties)

We can expand our own experience by finding out more about the human experiences of others – their struggles, lessons, emotional responses, and aspirations.

Authors are the gatekeepers to the lives they

explore. Harold Bloom, a well-known literature professor at Yale, has written many books about exciting authors. His book "Shakespeare, The Invention of the Human" claims that the playwright's vocabulary of 22,000 words made him well equipped to express the diverse experience of humankind. Therefore, according to Bloom, Shakespeare "invented the human," or at least a more complete definition of humanness as communicated through written storytelling.

In an interview published in 1995, Bloom reflected on the great authors of the Western world, stating the importance of reading and studying Shakespeare, Dante, Chaucer, and Cervantes. He said of these authors, "They provide an intellectual, I dare say, a spiritual value which has nothing to do with organized religion or the history of institutional belief… They tell us things we couldn't possibly know without them, and they reform our minds. They make us more vital." Indeed, Bloom defines humanness using the stories and writings of authors rather than his own life story, which proves how much the authors Bloom studied are a part of him.

Shakespeare's quotes reflect a deep understanding of humanness that resonates with our lives today. For example:

- "There is nothing good or bad; only thinking makes it so." —Hamlet

- "Hell is empty, and the devils are here." —The Tempest

- "Though this be madness, yet there is a method in it." — Hamlet

- "All that glistens is not gold." —The Merchant of Venice

- "To thine own self be true, and it must follow, as the night the day, thou canst not then be false to any man."—Hamlet

The meaning of life is much more than our daily experiences, and by reading, we can learn from others' experiences without having to endure them. For example, Hyeonseo Lee's "The Girl with Seven Names: Escape from North Korea" gave me a perspective of what it's like living under a totalitarian regime without suffering the personal experience myself. By embracing nonfiction accounts of others, you, too, can be a witness to many kinds of lives.

Even fiction brings us insight into our humanness. The suspense and twisting plots of fiction writer Lee Child in his "Jack Reacher" series take us to places we would never go and into situations we would never find ourselves. Instead, we find excitement, empathy, and emotional experiences in fiction.

Poetry can also challenge the status quo in our lives and, by doing so, improve the human condition of all people. For example, the work of Maya Angelou exposes the plights and triumphs of marginalized people fighting for equality and justice.

By reading, the knowledge learned through hearing others' stories gives meaning to our lives and inspires us to reach for more.

Chapter 12: Why Inspiration Is So Important

You look inward to tell your own story and outward to learn from others. Sometimes, you may have felt inspired or influenced mentally and emotionally to do something creative. But what is the purpose of being inspired?

Inspiration is energy that channels you toward a goal, pulling you along and motivating you. With some inspiration, it is easier to act on what you want.

A highly motivated person takes an idea into the real world and won't let anybody interfere with them. That's the person who isn't going to stop as obstacles inevitably arise. They keep going.

By living your life open-mindedly to other perspectives and our shared humanity, you can be equipped to adapt once pitfalls stand in your path.

However, motivation alone can't help you along life's journey—the inspiration working with motivation grounds you in the real world.

Ways to Find That Coveted Inspiration

This list of 25 sources for inspiration concludes with, **"You are the source of your inspiration."** This acknowledges that only you and your perception can feel inspired. You own it.

How you feel when you listen to music will not be created by the music but by how the music influences you. Instead, you recreate yourself as your inspiration finds new ways to see your experiences.

- Listen to music

- Dance

- Close your eyes for several minutes or

more in the daytime

- Watch an excellent symphony conductor conduct
- Listen and watch a great drummer drive a bands performance
- Read books
- Pick a subject to research
- Go for a walk
- Go for a run
- Climb a mountain
- Walk in the forest and trees
- Sit by a running stream and listen
- Walk barefoot on the grass
- Lay on the grass and watch the clouds
- Climb a mountain
- Listen to the wind blow through the leaves
- Meditate and listen to silence.
- Listen to your audience
- Spend time with your family and friends
- Go to a favorite place
- Spend time looking at art

- Daydream
- Sing aloud to your favorite songs
- Engage with mentors and teachers
- **You are the source of your inspiration**

How To Channel This Inspiration into Building Your Career

"Burnout" in a career is a real thing.

"The Great Resignation" revealed how a significant portion of the labor force quit or wanted to resign to try something else. The reported reasons include boredom at work, anxiety, fatigue, depression, frustration, difficulty concentrating, lack of creativity, and loss of trust.

I was talking with an old friend about his successful career, and he told me that he felt his longevity in his industry was seen as a negative, not a positive, by some in his field, and he had begun to think it was true. How could this be? He and others should view his vast experience as "added wisdom" gained by trial and error. His viewpoint spoke loudly to his burnout, but is this what years of work can lead to?

The dictionary definition of burnout is "the end of the powered stage in a rocket's flight when the propellant has been used up." With people, much energy pursuing various goals is spent, and when people are burned out, they feel somewhat used up and complacent.

You can hear the burnout in someone saying, "We tried that once before, and it didn't work, so it won't work now." My friend worked in the food service industry, and like many industries, it is dynamic – customers' preferences change. That should present challenges and opportunities, forcing us to rethink what we "always knew."

I advised my friend to become a student in his industry. Think of new approaches or new ways to use old products and concepts. This will provide you with renewed energy. As a veteran, you shouldn't worry about making a mistake. I told him that he, of all people, should know that a failure or setback is an opportunity. So when we start worrying about burnout, we should stop thinking about the past and look toward the future.

As business analyst and author Peter Drucker has said, "The best way to predict the future is to create it."

Chapter 13: Figuring Out Your Purpose

Mark Twain said, *"The two most important days in your life are the day you were born and the day you find out why."*

Why are we here? You may have asked yourself this once or twice. Is our life's purpose to be happy? Perhaps, and there's some logic to it.

Newborns seek happiness, and that is the primary purpose of their lives. But as they grow older, they recognize that others provide the things that lead to happiness. A child loves because he is loved first and feels the love from others before understanding it.

Higher self-esteem improves academic performance and better parent-child communication. On the other hand, children who do not have affectionate parents tend to have fewer positive outcomes on these measures.

The lesson is that those who consistently help others are happy and less likely to overcome self-imposed obstacles like stress. The subsequent experiences they have then result in their improved mental health.

So, I pose the question again - is our purpose to be happy or help others? The two feed each other. As adults, we serve each other in our lives and community, resulting in sustained, meaningful happiness.

> *There is no exercise better for the heart than reaching down and lifting people up."*

– John Holme

In Conclusion, The Power of Gratitude

All the inspiration and motivation in the world can't stop negative emotions like doubt and insecurity from creeping in occasionally. You may feel overwhelmed at times, perhaps even hopeless.

But there is an emotion we can choose to have and embrace to balance the darkness out. "Gratitude is an emotion that grounds us and is a great way to balance out the negative mindset that uncertainty engenders," said Dr. Guy Winch, author of the book "Emotional First Aid."

The future undoubtedly holds uncertainty, and often, that uncertainty can instill fear in us, seizing us into inaction.

Feeling closer and more connected to others helps motivate and sustain our efforts at self-improvement. When we're inspired by negative emotions, such as bitterness, resentment, or revenge, it is nearly impossible to maintain efforts to change positively. We will fail to find happiness if the motivation is achieved through negative means. Therefore, gratitude precedes happiness. Gratitude results in being willing and ready to show appreciation and return kindness. It brings a warm feeling of gratitude toward the world or specific individuals.

Gratitude helps people feel more positive emotions, feel more alive, express more compassion, relish good experiences, improve their health, deal with adversity, and build strong relationships.

With gratitude, you will be inspired to serve others. Happiness is found when your service is performed, not expecting something in return, and if you intend to help and lessen other people's misery.

So, if you're miserable in your job, feeling stuck in life, and stressed over your future, don't be surprised when you finally discover your calling after focusing on helping others rather than yourself.

With gratitude and this perspective, you will find that you're not alone. Everyone needs help sometimes, and the service is available to you, too, if you're strong enough to ask for it.

Your personal development takes one step and one day at a time, but by being actively curious about yourself and others while keeping a perspective of gratitude, that murky job search or journey toward happiness will become clearer before your eyes like a dark cloud making way for the bright sunshine.

"It is not joy that makes us grateful; it is gratitude that makes us joyful."

- David Steindl-Rast.

How to Contact the Author

Brent.M.Jones@connectedeventsmatter.com

About the Author

Brent M. Jones is a career development coach, consultant, author, and past Senior Business Executive. For years, Brent has been dedicated to motivating and educating people. He has helped hundreds of candidates to reevaluate themselves for a career change and acquire the skills needed for the job they desire while learning to navigate the marketplace.

True to the words, "Practice what you Preach" Brent reinvented himself while assisting people in finding new jobs and realized the importance of networking and relationships in their true sense. He has carefully curated detailed and real-life insights on succeeding in job seeking with actionable advice. Brent believes in adapting to the changes with innovative strategies that will help people follow their passion and attain success while inspiring them to listen to their inner voices.

Be passionate about improving. Be passionate about helping others. Listen to your feelings.

Amazon Author Page

amazon.com/author/brentjones

Book Reviews

Please consider leaving a review on this book on the Amazon review section. Reviews are essential to enable a book to move ahead and be read by more readers, and your help will be appreciated.

Authors Website

connectedeventsmatter.com

Thank you for Reading.

Other Books by Brent M. Jones

Mastering the Art of Communication: The Power of Precision in Language"

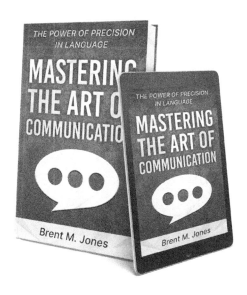

Work Matters: It Takes Technology, Insight, and Strategies for Job Seekers In This Evolving World

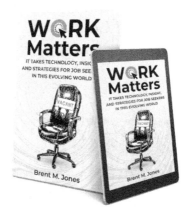

Embrace Life's Randomness: Your Path to Personal Reinvention and Positive Change

Networking With a Purpose: The Informational Interview, Its Use and Why it is a Valuable Tool

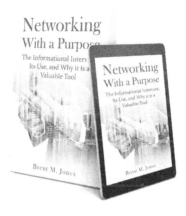

The Human Factor: How Finding Your Dream Job Starts by Getting to Know Yourself

Why Life Stories Change: Are We the Result of Chance or Circumstance

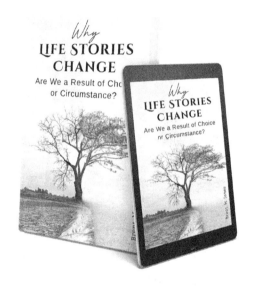

Made in the USA
Las Vegas, NV
08 April 2024

88404642R00049